I AM

Affirmation Journal to
TransformU

I am...

THE AFFIRMATION JOURNAL TO *TransformU*

LaTonya Renee

I Am...The Affirmation Journal to TransformU

Copyright © 2017 by **LaTonya Renee**

All rights reserved. No part of this publication may be reproduced, distributed or transmitted in any form or by any means, without prior written permission.

For Information Contact: LaTonya Renee
www.latonyarenee.com

Published by LaTonya Renee

Book cover designed by P2P Branded @ http://www.p2pbranded.com

Editing and interior design by Trudi Batiste

ISBN-978-1977806987   ISBN-101977806988

I would like to thank God for birthing this book inside of me and for walking with me throughout this entire process.

Dedication

I dedicate this book to my three beautiful children: Brandon, Janelle, and Javon. Also, to my grandchildren: Jaquan, Raelle, Neal, Sarenity and Braxton; who continue to inspire me to be a living sacrifice, to break mediocracy and live a life by design

not default.

Acknowledgements

To my mother Delores Smith, my sisters Angela Albright and Tiffany Carter; family support is priceless, and I could not be the person I am without your unwavering support of everything I do. I appreciate the unconditional love you show me daily, as well as the bond we share. Your love is without condition, not only in the good times but most of all through the difficult times.

To my late brother Curtis Albright, I miss you dearly. We never imagined living this life without you. Your passing ignited our love for one another and taught us not to take the short time that we have for granted. You've shown me how to "use what's in my hands," the gifts and talents God blessed me with to bless humanity.

I Love You. Love Never Dies.

To my Power Circle: Thank you for continuing to Push, Encourage and to Empower me to walk into my greatness.

I Love you.

LaTonya Renee

The Power of Affirmations

I'm so excited that you've decided to purchase my "I Am... The Affirmation Journal to TransformU." That tells me that you are ready to make some serious changes about your future and the future of your family. You know what else is awesome about that? *"It only takes one person."* Yes, one person can change the trajectory of an entire household, family, or community. I know because it happened for me and my family. I'm still working on extended family and community, but it's a start.

According to Louise Hay, an affirmation opens the door. It's a beginning point on the path to change. You're saying to your subconscious mind: *"I am taking responsibility. I am aware that there is something I can do to change."* When I talk about *doing affirmations,* I am consciously choosing words that will either help *eliminate* something from your life or help *create* something new in your life.

Affirmations are positive statements that describe a desired situation or goal, and the process causes the subconscious mind to strive and to work on your statement coming true. By using this process consciously and intently, you influence your subconscious mind and in turn, it transforms your habits, behaviors, attitude and reactions. Affirmations reshape your external life repeatedly until they are impressed upon the subconscious mind to make it positive.

I need for you to understand how powerful the mind is. What you think about all day and what you allow to enter your ear gate has direct effect on the way you think. To have a positive life, (taking a different approach to your circumstances) you must become accustomed to speaking positivity through affirmations into your life. Your mind is naturally attracted to the negative. For example, it is natural that when you have a problem with your health, relationships, or finances to focus, on all the negative components of the situation. All people see is the negative of what's going on. Naturally, they replay it over and over with the negative as the primary focus. Sometimes the details of your situation are so painful, the frustration becomes so overwhelming, it slips into every area of your life. People often never focus on the good or the future. Their future can turn out much better than what they are currently experiencing. Once you develop the habit of using affirmations, you will learn how to speak your way out of your situations, when all you see with your natural eye is the negative. It takes twenty-one days to break a habit. There is no better day than today to start. When you can change the way you think, you can change your entire life.

"As a man thinketh so is he." Proverbs 23:7

LaTonya Renee

The Set-Up

Growing up, I was never told about speaking positive affirmations. I had never heard of affirmations, let alone knew what it meant to speak them. No one around me was speaking affirmations. Everyone around me was basically surviving, day to day survival, week to week and paycheck to paycheck. My life was the exact picture of my environment. I became a teenage mother who was forced to drop out of school because I didn't have childcare. I finally managed to secure childcare; however, the issue then became transportation. During that period in time, it felt like *"you're damned if you do and damned if you don't."* The adults in my life consisted of family and friends. They couldn't help me with resources or information. Remember, I stated that everyone was in survival mode. I asked family and friends to help with my schedule of getting my children to school so I wouldn't be tardy or miss school altogether. Some started out with good intentions, they would forget, or simply did not want to be committed to the responsibility. Some made promises they never kept, and some just flat out said *"NO"*.

I can remember getting up and getting my children and myself ready for the day only to sit for hours hoping and wishing my ride would show up. I can also remember asking a family member, '*Will you please just take my daughter to school?*' That would have given me enough time to catch the school bus. Their response to me was, *"I don't have time for that."* Getting high was the only thing on their agenda for the day, so there was no time to haul a child around at 7:00 a.m. There were days I would get off to a good start, get my children to daycare and then make it to school. There were other days my children made it to daycare; however, I was flat out of luck. Some days none of us made it. Surviving meant my problems were *my* problems and every man for themselves.

It was my senior year of high school, so you'd think my school attendance would have created some immediate concerns. It didn't seem to bother a soul. Life moved right along as normal!!! It appeared I'd made my own bed and I was the only one that would have to lie in it. I was on my own. I remember desperately wanting to finish school. I was already feeling disgusted with the decisions I made-- becoming a mother at 17 years old, not once but twice. I was frantically trying to get this school situation right, so I could say I accomplished something positive not just for myself, but also my children.

I remember having one of the nicest guidance counselors at East Forsyth, Mrs. Hall. She fought hard for me to stay in traditional school; however, the principal at that time wouldn't go for it. Mrs. Hall and the principal came to an agreement. I had to enroll in an alternative school, something that I absolutely hated. During my entire years of going to school, I was never a problem child; to have to go to an alternative school crushed my spirit. It felt like in some way it meant that I was bad, no-good, and non-existent. Mrs. Hall told me that according to the principle, I would have to attend the alternative school from September thru December. That gave me an opportunity to catch-up on the assignments that I had missed. After getting over my pity-party I put on my big girl panties and toughed it out. All I wanted to do was to return to school with my peers and graduate. I begin putting all my efforts into studying and getting my work completed and caught up. I completed every assignment and then some. I was ecstatic that I would be returning to East Forsyth after the holidays. January came, and I was not only thrilled about returning to school, but also excited that I could now participate in all the senior activities alongside my peers. I will never forget returning to school, work completed, happy, daycare situation under control and ready to finish out those last five months of this high school journey. I can remember it so vividly, as I sat in Mrs. Hall's office that day when she told me *"I'm sorry LaTonya, the principal is not going to allow you to return to school."* I was baffled!

"What do you mean Mrs. Hall? I put in the work. Every assignment was done and turned in on time with a "C" or better. What happened? I've completed all the requirements that she imposed on me to come back." Mrs. Hall stated, *"I'm unsure why she changed her mind."*

She proceeded to say to me that if I were of a different race or from a different neighborhood, I would be back to school with no problem. Mrs. Hall was just as upset and as angry as I was. She stated how students from higher socio-economic backgrounds that have committed offenses that would uphold being expelled are allowed to walk on this campus. The difference was their parents came to the school, supported the school's athletes, PTA, and fundraisers. Here I was the only one advocating for my return to school outside of my guidance counselor, Mrs. Hall. It was easy for the principal to deny me access to finish my education based on the community I came from and what I believe she considered to be "just another statistic." This was one of my earlier experiences of being marginalized. I felt powerless. I was a minority, teenage mother with no outside support against a Caucasian principal. At that moment in my mind I didn't stand a chance.

Once again, my spirit was crushed. I was just thrown a blow that made me feel like I was the dirt and trash that accumulates under the bottom of a worn-out shoe. The tears rained down like a flood for days, weeks and months thereafter. Not only was I a high school drop-out, but also a teenage mother, so I had not one, but two labels. I felt everyone could clearly see the enormous scarlet "A" for alternative that was spray painted on my back.

With only five months left to graduate, I never returned to public high school after that day. I did the next best thing I knew to do; I went to work full-time making minimum wage at Davis department store in downtown Winston-Salem, North Carolina.

"There is just as much to be learned from failure as there is success."

Paradigm Shift

Within the next year or two, I obtained my GED through the local community college. It took me many years to get over the fact that I did not graduate from high school with my peers. For so many years during graduation season, I'd become depressed and never celebrated anyone else's accomplishments during that time. The devastating emotions of that experience added fuel to my insecurities and low self-esteem. In 1997, I enrolled in the local community college's Criminal Justice program. During this time, I still did not know anything about affirmations, but I knew that I needed to do something different. It was either continue to conform to what everyone around me was doing or go in the opposite direction. I chose to go in the opposite direction.

I was still working to fill an internal void with external accomplishments. Statics nearly kept me from receiving my 2-year Associate degree, but I made it. Earning that degree motivated me to continue the road to higher education. Still searching, for acceptance, joy and validation, I went on to enroll in Winston-Salem State University. At WSSU, I completed my bachelor's degree in Sociology. Let me tell you, the week of graduation after completing all the exit confirmations, I was told

I AM...

I was not going to graduate. *What you say sir/ma'am?* After shedding some tears, showing up in various offices and running down documentation, I was approved to graduate. I was not completely relaxed until the day of rehearsal when I heard my name being called... that was my confirmation.

As you can see my experiences with obtaining any form of education has been a major struggle. I now know God was working on my internal muscles, my faith muscles, self-esteem muscle and courage muscle. Some hurts we've experienced in life can take a lifetime to recover. We were unaware that we struggled because we never, confronted, accepted, and forgave ourselves or others for the hurt that happened many years ago. Instead of moving forward and resolving the issue, we allow the pain and hurt to fester, and it grows like cancer causing emotional and even psychological issues.

> *Your vision will become clear only when you look into your heart. Who looks outside, dreams. Who looks inside awakens.*
> *Carl Gustav Jung*

Purpose Revealed

Once again, I decided to enroll in a higher learning program. It was to obtain my master's degree. I figured this would help me to earn more money in my career.

Earning a master's degree would look attractive on my resume, and society said it would allow me to *strive* instead of surviving. I so desperately wanted to strive. I needed to show people like the principal at East Forsyth that I'm not a statistic; I turned out to be a good person, a good mother and I'm educated. I continually ran like hell away from the environment that raised me, into one that seemed to never accept me. And oh yeah, did I mention I still had the empty void in the pit of my stomach that is the dwelling place for low self-esteem and the need to fit in? Yep, it was still there after 20 plus years.

There's a saying that goes *"Sometimes in life, your situation will keep repeating itself until you learn the lesson."* I guess I just loved or needed some good old criticism to build my self-esteem muscle. North Carolina A&T was where I received the internal training I needed to finally get over being a high school dropout, and to break the vicious cycle I was repeating. There, at North Carolina A&T State University while earning my master's degree, is where I learned the power of affirmations. That was a life-changing journey for me. That's where I

I AM...

accepted that I was powerful, I was worthy, and I already had everything I needed on the inside of me.

I was on top of world when I received the acceptance letter to A&T. I was accepted to one of the nation's top HBCU's in their Master's Community Counseling program. For me, it was prestigious and only a small percentage of people held a master's degree, and I wanted to be in that group of individuals. The first year and a half was, as they say, "Peaches and Cream." I collaborated with some awesome people and I maintained an A-B average. My world began to unravel in 2012. I found myself after 14 years of marriage going through divorce, a health scare and to top it all off, my grades began take a dive. Out of everything that was going wrong in my life, my educational career was the most devastating for me.

After being in graduate school for 2 years, always active and respectful, I was being told over the phone that I could no longer be a student in the counseling program. I remember having the same devastating feelings that I had in January 1988. I felt like an absolute failure. Not only had my marriage failed, but I'd also failed out of graduate school. I remember replaying over and over again how I was going to explain this to my adult children, my peers, my family and my co-workers. I'll never forget leaving work that Tuesday and crying all the way home. I cried as I prepared myself for a meeting with my partners. I cried all the way to the meeting. Prior to everyone arriving I dried my face, painted on a smile and forged my way through, smiling on the outside and devastated on the inside. As soon as the meeting was over, and I reached my car, the tears began to flow uncontrollably. That was the beginning of many tear-filled nights. Some nights I cried myself to sleep, while others I cried for the entire night. For the next several days, my attempts to meet with advisors and department heads were unsuccessful. Only after I became persistent and reached out to the office for student services did I receive a call back. That Friday at around

4:00 p.m., the department head left me a message. I immediately called back.

She said, "*I heard you were looking for me.*" I responded, "Yes ma'am." She replied, *"If you want to see me, you need to be here by 5:00p.m."*

It's Friday at 4:00p.m., in the afternoon, rush hour is about to begin and I'm approximately 45-50 minutes away from Greensboro. Without hesitation, I dropped everything and proceeded to my car and headed to the campus of A&T. Once in her office, I eagerly begin to plead my case, the adversities that were going on in my life, the divorce and health issues. I pointed out that I had maintained an A-B average prior to my grades dropping. In the mist of my explanation, I begin crying. Receiving this degree was going to be the end of just surviving in life. This degree was going to give me the ax to cut the ties to my difficult past…so, I thought. Not any of what I'd said evoked her having any sympathy for me. She used everything I said against me. She stated, *"I don't think your stable enough to complete the program."* Next, she asked if I was receiving any financial assistance to attend school. She then went on to say that her recommendation is that I withdraw from school the following day. *"Don't wait. Go ahead and take care of this immediately",* she stated. She assured me that I could re-enroll in the program in about a year. She had absolutely no intention of allowing me to remain a part of the counseling program. I left the office feeling even worse than when I arrived. There I was again feeling like that 17-year-old girl that was unable to graduate high school with her peers--powerless without a voice and once more being forced to give up on her education, to leave and never come back.

Maybe I wasn't good enough to have a master's Degree. The negative chatter in my head beat my self-esteem so low, it was hard to face my own image in the mirror. I was disappointed in myself. You're trying to be something you know nothing about. Your

I AM...

family only knows struggle, lack, and defeat. They only know how to live a life of survival, not thriving. You have failed once again. I managed to replay this day after day and week after week, until one night during one of my crying episodes, God covered me with so much love, grace and forgiveness. God's love gave me so much strength and courage that I made the decision to not withdraw from school. I decided to take a break from school. I decided to take a break for one semester before going back. Although I was a fully-grown woman on the outside, I was still the young, high school dropout, teenage mother that needed acceptance on the inside. The semester I sat out allowed me to build up my internal muscle, courage, and self-esteem. I still needed to get permission. The department head's signature was the only approval I needed to stay in school. I decided to wait until after the Christmas holiday before confronting her again. During that time away from class, I worked specifically on my thought life. I empowered myself through the Word of God and Positive Affirmations. My home was covered with sticky notes in my bedroom, bathroom, kitchen, and car. I had to transform the way I thought about my situation. I spoke those affirmations, morning, noon and night along with the Word of God until I built up my inner muscles, my confidence muscle, my courage muscle and my self-esteem muscle.

    I intentionally waited until after the Christmas break to schedule an appointment with the department head. I figured that time with family, much needed rest, and the holiday atmosphere could prick even the hardest heart. The meeting was not about her it was about me and the strength that I had built internally. No longer was I going to appear like the weak pawn that was in her office the semester before. I was prepared for a "no" but expecting a "yes". My plan was to again plead my case boldly, acknowledging the issues, but this time offering a solution as well. This time my internal being was so strong until my own emotions had no choice to stay at bay. This meeting will be the direct opposite of the last meeting "and it was".

I may have looked like the same person on the outside, however, I was a much different person on the inside. I requested another meeting with the department head and she surprisingly agreed. This time I kept my emotions in check, this time I felt in control of the meeting and refused to back down from my goal, which was to be allowed to stay in school. I pointed out my mistakes, while showing her that I was only a few classes shy of graduating. Although I had failed two classes with a 'C,' I still maintained a passing GPA. She acknowledged that I must have a strong faith in God, because it showed, and it was also working in my favor. She agreed to allow me to stay in school. The stipulation was, I had to transfer from the Counseling program into the Adult Education Program. Yeah, she allowed me to continue my education journey, but she made it clear that I was basically starting over. Did she really mean two years gone down the drain? I showed up to every class determined that somehow some way this had to turn in favor.

Although I was overwhelmed with joy that I was going to finish school my mind continued to try and torment me. Torn between just being grateful to be in school and the assimilation into a new program, with new cohorts. I often wondered why, how and what just happened. My journey began to look so different from how it started; it appeared that God rerouted the GPS system, from where I planned. I had developed a good plan, but God has something so much greater in store for me. I met the best, compassionate classmates, advisors and department heads. They made me feel right at home in the Education Department, and I jumped right in as if I had been there all along. The professors encouraged and stretched me into being an exemplary student despite my personal struggles.

The fall of 2014, my advisor and I was going over my transcript and I began to explain my situation. She said, *"you only need to complete your internship and one other class, and you're done".* She adjusted my paperwork signed off on it and I was on my way. I always say she was my "ram in the bush". I'm proud to say December 2014, I graduated with a Masters in Adult Education with a concentration in community counseling, nearly two master's degrees. The devil thought he had me again, but this time I put up a fight, a fight that started in my mind, how I saw myself… no longer a victim but victorious.

Just like during my past educational journey's, the enemy attempted to destroy my spirit. The enemy will use the same old tactics, pulling back old scabs from old wounds pouring in fear, doubt and frustration. With so much calamity going on it was easier to give in and give up, however I knew deep down no matter what it looked like, I was the only one that could change my situation. Looking back, I understand that everything I went through was all for my good. I needed a disruption in order to build my faith muscles, and my courage muscles. Leaning on my faith and speaking affirmations gave me the tenacity to keep going forward in the midst of chaos. I'm going to need that strength, courage and focus for where God is taking me. Every level is going to require a deeper level of trust, faith and resilience.

> ***Success is not final; failure is not fatal: it is the courage to continue that counts."***
> ***- Winston Churchill.***

Watch your thoughts, they become words. Watch your words, they become actions. Watch your actions, they become habits. Watch your habits, they become your

LaTonya Renee

character. Watch your character, it becomes your destiny.

- Cindy Trimm

I AM...

HOW TO USE THIS JOURNAL

This affirmation journal is set up with an affirmation along with a biblical scripture (NIV) that supports each one. I encourage you to immerse yourself in each affirmation as well as each scripture for as long as you need to.

You can never grow bigger than your thoughts, decide to put in the work; to change your current belief system. Research your old belief systems, then challenge yourself to create new belief systems.

Journaling your new belief system will reaffirm what you want to see happen in your thought life. Journaling will also trigger you to give more focus and attention to your affirmations.

I pray you enjoy.

I am ... Affirmation Journal to *Transform U*

I AM ENOUGH!

The enemy constantly tries to plant seeds of lack in your mind. Thoughts that continually tell you that you need more education, more money, a different look or a new job. The goal is to keep you searching outside of yourself for what you have inside of you to succeed in life. Don't waste one more day, month or year searching for validation. You are enough!

You are made worthy through the blood of Jesus Christ!

"Being confident of this, that he who begins a good work in you will carry it out to completion until the day of Christ Jesus"

Philippians 1:6

I AM CAPABLE OF ACHIEVING MY GOALS.

I always say, "how bad do you want it?" Reaching goals in your personal, professional and business life is a test of faith. When you get to the point that giving up is not an option.

You have already won, so expect to win!!

"Let us not become weary in doing good, for at the proper time we will reap a harvest if we do not give up."

Galatians 6:9

I AM COMMITTED TO BEING A BETTER PERSON THAN I WAS YESTERDAY; HEALTHIER THOUGHTS, IMPROVED DECISIONS AND BIGGER ACTIONS.

When you heighten your commitment level to better yourself, thoughts, and actions, the results will be life changing. Opportunities will suddenly find you, relationships will become reciprocal. Informed decisions will determine great destinations. Your overall quality of life will begin to manifest into something that you never imagined.

When you work on yourself first you open yourself up to everything you're looking for to find you.

Be very careful, then, how you live—not as unwise but as wise"

Ephesians 5:15

I AM GRATEFUL THAT MONEY COMES TO ME IN INCREASING QUANTITIES FROM MANY SOURCES ON A CONTINUOUS BASIS.

If you have been programmed to go to work and attempt to have a full life off of one stream of income, that may not be realistic in this day and time. If you intend on leaving a legacy, you must have multiple streams. I challenge you to uncover those gifts and talents buried inside of you. Your God given talents will transfer into streams of income. Your talents are needed in the world and people will pay you if you use them.

Diversify your streams.

"A river watering the garden flowed from Eden; from there it was separated into four headwaters"

Genesis 2:10

I HAVE THE POWER TO ATTRACT MONEY!

"Money is the root of all evil." "Money doesn't grow on trees." You must rid yourself of the old limited belief systems about money, generational habits and beliefs about money that have been passed down for generations.

There is no doubt that God as intended us to have wealth. You must speak to your money. You are the master and money is your servant.

You must tell money when to come and when to go.

But remember the Lord your God, for it is he who gives you the ability to produce wealth, and so confirms his covenant, which he swore to your ancestors, as it is today."

Deuteronomy 8:18

I AM PROUD OF MYSELF!

Get in the habit of celebrating yourself. Even the smallest accomplishments deserve recognition. Celebrating the small and medium wins keeps you motivated to work toward big wins. You're doing a good job!

Don't stop, keep going!

"A happy heart makes the face cheerful, but heartache crushes the spirit."

Proverbs 15:13

I AM EXCITED ABOUT THE PERSON I AM BECOMING!

It's so exciting when our eyes have been opened and our minds transformed. Then, is when we truly begin to live a purposed filled life according to what God has planned for us. Being transformed is a beautiful life long journey that only the Heavenly Father can give.

Continue to evolve and you will forever be excited about the gifts and talents you have on the inside waiting to make their entrance into the world.

"Do not conform to the pattern of this world but be transformed by the renewing of your mind. Then you will be able to test and approve what God's will is his good, pleasing and perfect will."

Romans 12:2

> **MY ABILITY TO CONQUER MY CHALLENGES IS LIMITLESS. MY POTENTIAL TO SUCCEED IS UNLIMITED.**

God gives strength that goes beyond what we understand in the natural. Our ability to overcome some of life's most difficult challenges is not our own.

Out of our challenges often comes our biggest victories.

"I can do all this through him who gives me strength."

Philippians 4:13

> **MY GIFTS ARE VALUABLE AND WANTED. THERE IS NO LIMIT TO THEIR ABUNDANCE.**

People often look to education to make them successful; however, the bible says, "You were born with God given gifts, talents and abilities." Those gifts and talents are not for you to keep hidden. You are to develop those gifts and present them to the world.

Gifts are a part of God's master plan for humanity. Your gifts are the key to your success.

"A gift opens the way and ushers the giver into the presence of the great"

Proverbs 18:16

I'M NOT DOING ANYTHING WRONG.
I'M DOING SOMETHING NEW.

Different; out of the ordinary or change, can often times bring about discomfort and worry. You second guess your ability to make accurate decisions concerning your life.

I promise you if you can bear the discomfort, ridicule and stress of change, God will guide you right into a promise land of blessings.

"The LORD had said to Abram, "Go from your country, your people and your father's household to the land I will show you."

*"I will make you into a great nation,
and I will bless you;
I will make your name great,
and you will be a blessing
I will bless those who bless you,
and whoever curses you I will curse;
and all peoples on earth
will be blessed through you."*

Genesis 12:1-3

I AM INVESTING IN MYSELF BECAUSE I'M WORTH IT.

Depending on your own knowledge will only get you so far in life. You are winning when you understand the value of investing in a multitude of wise counsel. Ensure that you build a team of individuals that support you through the good times, as well as help you maneuver through the bad times.

Your investment in people catapults your purpose to a while other level.

"Plans fail for lack of counsel, but with many advisers they succeed."

Proverbs 15:22

EVERYDAY I TAKE POSITIVE ACTION TOWARDS MY GOALS.

I believe prayer changes our situations and as believers, we must pray. Your desires can not come to fruition on prayer alone. We must take action. Action is one of the greatest acts of faith we can display that our belief in God is real. We must be vigilant in our daily actions even when the circumstances seem overwhelming. You must have a plan and act on your plan.

#Pray&Plan #Plan&Pray

"In the same way, faith by itself, if not accomplished with action, is dead."

James 2:17

BECAUSE I BELIEVE IN MY GOALS, I ACHIEVE MY GOALS.

You must believe in your goals even when the plans go against human reason or human experience. When you plan out your goals, ask in faith without a shadow of a doubt. No matter the outcome every situation will work out in your favor.

Whenever your belief system is working at its highest capacity, there is nothing that you cannot accomplish.

"But when you ask, you must believe and not doubt, because the one who doubts is like a wave of the sea, blown and tossed by the wind."

James 1:6

MOTIVATION COMES FROM THE INSIDE. I AM MY OWN MOTIVATOR.

It takes much more effort to stay negative, angry & hostile rather than to be synched with a positive one. Empowering your mind and soul daily with positivity will fuel the motivation internally and will show up externally. A positive attitude gives you power over your circumstances, instead of your circumstances having power over you.

A motivated person is attractive and will attract other positive people into their lives.

"You will keep in perfect peace those whose minds are steadfast, because they trust in you."

Isaiah 26:3

I AM LETTING GO OF EVERYTHING AND EVERYONE THAT NO LONGER SERVES ME.

Unfortunately, when relationships and places you frequent no longer have any value in your life, it's time to let go. It doesn't mean that those people or places are bad; however, you have to make room. When you are walking towards your destiny, new relationships that bring substance and value for your purpose will have to be formed. As difficult as this can be for many people, the long-term outcome is priceless. It's a part of trusting God.

You're winning when you can move forward!

***"Forget the former things;
do not dwell on the past".***

Isaiah 43:18

I AM COMFORTABLE BEING UNCOMFORTABLE.

Being uncomfortable is part of growth. God didn't create us to be comfortable, average, or just barely get by. If you never want to experience being uncomfortable, or being stretched, you lose the chance to have what God has in store for you. God allows us to be in uncomfortable places to prepare us for our next position.

There is a new world waiting for you on the other side of your comfort zone.

"Have I not commanded you? Be strong and courageous. Do not be afraid; do not be discouraged, for the LORD your God will be with you wherever you go."

Joshua 1:9

I LOVE CHANGING AND ADJUSTING MYSELF TO NEW SITUATIONS.

Most people would rather live their lives repeating the same behaviors day in and day out, and the entire time expecting to see a positive change in their lives. I'm here to tell you change is good and God loves those who will take risk. If you just Look around social media and do a survey of the individuals that step out on faith and take risks verses the people that never take any risks, the risk takers are actively working toward living a life they desire. The people that repeat the same behaviors are living life on life's terms.

I am a risk taker!

"By faith Abraham, when called to go to a place he would later receive as his inheritance, obeyed and went, even though he did not know where he was going."

Hebrews 11:8

I AM A GIVER OF GOD'S VISION TO HELP THOSE IN NEED.

There have been many, including myself, that have been in circumstances where we needed someone to bless us through giving, prayer, or shelter. Our blessings will be based upon our willingness to help others. The great revelation about giving is "we cannot out give God". His blessing is infinite.

The more we give from a cheerful heart expecting nothing in return other than to fulfill gods purpose to take care of the kingdom and help those in need, the more we can expect for our homes and families to be blessed.

"Give, and it will given to you. A good measure, pressed down, shaken together and running over will be poured into your lap. For with the measure you use, it will be measured to you."

Luke 6:38

I AM MY OWN RESCUE.

When you know better, you do better. No one is exempt from falling prey to unfavorable circumstances. There is nothing new under the sun. you can recover, Reset and regain yourself with determination and discipline.

You are your own rescue. no one can save you from you but you.

"No temptation has overtaken you except what is common to mankind. And God is faithful; he will not let you be tempted beyond what you can bear. But when you are tempted, he will also provide a way out so that you can endure it."

1Corinthians 10:13

I FORGIVE MYSELF FOR ALL THE MISTAKES I HAVE MADE.

I know you have heard your elders say, "live long enough you will go through some type of adversity." Who hasn't found themselves in unfulfilling relationships, difficult careers, caught up in gossip that ruin peoples character or worse. You won't live this life without being confronted with situations that makes you want to crawl under a rock and hibernate. During these valley experiences, is when we find the most growth. The goal is deal with the experience, grow, learn and forgive others and yourself.

Grace and mercies are made new every day.

"And all are justified freely by his grace through the redemption that came by Christ Jesus."

Romans 3:24

I AM SURROUNDED BY LOVE.

When you get to the place where you understand that God loves you no matter what, a true unconditional love, no matter the numerous times you fail, or go back to a situation after you said you wouldn't. You will begin to live a life of freedom from guilt, shame and comparing yourself to others. Your past mistakes can no longer hold you hostage. God is no respecter of persons. You are loved just the same as the next person and you are privileged to all that God has for you. You will begin to love others the way God loves you.

What you give out will be what you get in return.

"Love is patient, love is kind. It does not envy, it does not boast, it is not proud. It does not dishonor others, it is not self-seeking, it is not easily angered, it keeps no record of wrongs. Love does not delight in evil but rejoices with the truth. It always protects always trust, always hopes, always perseveres."

1 Corinthians 13:4-7

I HAVE GOOD LOVING RELATIONSHIPS.

I have always lived by the motto "treat others like you want to be treated," fall in love with people who have your best interest at heart and learn to let go of unfulfilling relationships. You have to learn when their season in your life is over, so you can #makeroom for new relationships. When you are walking into a purpose driven life, you will begin to meet people who are pre-ordained to enhance your life. In return, you make their life better. Loving relationships begin to flow into your life naturally.

Be a good sibling, child, parent, friend spouse and it will be given to you.

"So, in everything, do to others what you would have them to do you, for this sums up the Law and the Prophets."

Matthew 7:12

MY BODY IS MY TEMPLE AND I TAKE GOOD CARE OF IT.

Your physical health is an important part of living a productive life. When you fill your body with excessive amounts of grease, fatty foods and sweets, you deplete energy; the energy you need to be productive. Once I started a regular exercise routine, I could tell a difference in my creativity to develop new ideas and the excitement and energy to accomplish them. Sexual intimacy can be a beautiful thing, but on the other side, sexual desires is one of the most difficult for humans to control. Your body is not meant to be shared with everyone.

God created us and it's God's property.

"Therefore, I urge you, brothers and sisters, in view of god's mercy, to offer your bodies as a living sacrifice, holy and pleasing to God. This is your true and proper worship."

Romans 12:1

MY EFFORTS ARE FRUITFUL ALL MY PLANS TURN OUT BETTER THAN I EXPECTED.

It's so exciting when your plan works out the way you want. It's even more exciting when God gets involved, your plans become even better than you could have imagined. When you give God something to work with (plans), it gives him an opportunity to do what only he can do.

Your plans are not only for you, but what God wants to see in his kingdom.

"Commit to the LORD whatever you do, and he will establish your plans."

Proverbs 16:3

I AM OPEN TO RECEIVE ALL THAT GOD HAS FOR ME.

God will do a new thing. New Strength, New Ideas, New Breakthroughs, New Blessings, New Peace, name it-and He will do it.

Trust with all your heart, believe without a doubt that anything is possible with God.

"See, I am doing a new thing!
Now it springs up; do you not perceive it?
I am making a way in the wilderness
and streams in the wasteland."

Isaiah 43:19

I AM POWERFUL! I AM BOLD! I AM BEAUTIFUL!

You are more powerful than you know, you have handled all of life's trials with humility and grace. You are bold enough to take control and design a life on your own terms. You are most beautiful when you are unafraid to be true to yourself.

Let the world know how Powerful, Bold and Beautiful you are!

"When I called, you answered me; you greatly emboldened me."

Psalm 138:3

I FORGIVE THOSE WHO HAVE HARMED ME IN THE PAST AND PEACEFULLY DETACH FROM THEM.

Sometimes we become prey to wolves in sheep's clothing. Your vulnerability can be seen from miles away and individuals will pounce on your weakness to make themselves feel strong. Your neediness is attractive to them looking to devour you mentally, financially and spiritually in order to make them feel good about themselves. Respect yourself enough to detach yourself from anything and anyone that is not making any positive deposits into your life.

Forgive yourself, forgive them; pray for yourself and them while you walk away!

Be kind and compassionate to one another, forgiving each other, just as in Christ God forgave you.

Ephesians 4:32

> **I AM WEALTHY. MY BANK ACCOUNT IS OVERFLOWING. I HAVE MORE THAN ENOUGH MONEY FOR MYSELF, TO HELP OTHERS, AND TO BUILD UP THE KINGDOM OF GOD.**

I am a firm believer that we are blessed to be a blessing. If you are financially blessed, don't hesitate to bless others, or organizations. If you are a successful business owner, mentor an inspiring business owner. If you are a great leader, teach someone how to lead. Use your gifts and talents to multiply God's purpose for humanity.

What you make happen for others God will make happen for you.

"But someone who does not know, and then does something wrong, will be punished only lightly. When someone has been given much, much will be required in return; and when someone has been entrusted with much, even more will be required."

Luke 12:48

TODAY, I ABANDON MY OLD HABITS AND TAKE UP NEW ONES.

The truth is this affirmation will take time, by no means is it easy, but it is doable. There are factors like environment and circle of influence that can keep you stagnate or propel you into developing new habits that change your life. The key is to Re-focus, Reposition and Renew.

When you make your goals priority, position yourself in arenas that cultivate the change you want to see. Your new habits will take on a life of their own.

"But if you fail to drive out the people who live in the land, those who remain will be like splinters in your eyes and thorns in your sides. They will harass you in the land where you live. And I will do to you what I had planned to do to them."

Numbers 33:55-56

I AM AN INFLUENCER, AND I SURROUND MYSELF WITH INFLUENCERS. MANY PEOPLE RECOGNIZE MY WORTH.

If you want to be an influencer, you must also be a leader. Followers typically get lost in the crowd. Influencers stay involved and they are always abreast of global trends. I believe influencers are a bit radical; they tend go against the norm. Being a life-long learner is essential for influencers. Influencers are confident and attract other confident influencers.

Continue to grow your mind and your skillset. There will be many people that will recognize your worth.

"In the same way, let your light shine before others, that they may see your good deeds and glorify your Father in heaven."

Matthew 5:16

I AM GRATEFUL!

Expressing gratitude and being grateful for the blessings you currently have will make room for more blessings. I am grateful for whatever state I'm in because I have learned the world can supply us with happiness, but only God can give joy. I'm grateful for change, I'm grateful for a renewed mind, I'm grateful I can find peace in a world full of chaos, I'm grateful for health, prosperity and a life of abundance. I'm grateful that God Doesn't Call the Qualified...God Qualifies the Called!

God will use the most unqualified people with all their flaws, weaknesses, & dysfunctional characteristics to create change, impact and empower others.

I Am Grateful!

I am not saying this because I am in need, for I have learned to be content whatever the circumstances.

Philippians 4:11

I AM _____?

In addition to empowering your mind with positive affirmations, here are 10 additional tips to overcome negative thinking:

1. Re-evaluate your current relationships.

2. Bring positivity to someone else's life.

3. Get an attitude of gratitude for what you have right now.

4. Visualize yourself out of your current situation into something you desire.

5. Make a vision board.

6. Write goals and work toward meeting them.

7. Workout.

8. Share your story. Someone needs to hear it.

9. Meditate.

10. Keep positive quotes around your living space.

ABOUT THE AUTHOR

LaTonya Renee is an author, public speaker, and transformational coach. Coming from a community of social dysfunction, she dodged drug abuse and incarceration only to succumb to negative choices and low self-worth. She overcame being a high school dropout, teenage pregnancy and divorce. Determined to fill a void in her life, she used her faith in God and education as a tool to propel her life into a new direction.

LaTonya uses experiences from her past and her job for over 17 years in the North Carolina Department of Public Safety Prison system. LaTonya's professional career consists of Staff Development Training & Outreach Specialist. She works with victims of crime and counsels incarcerated offenders, both male and female, as well as their families. LaTonya depends on God to help her Educate, Empower & Elevate others to find the internal change they desire in their lives. She believes that if you can change your mindset, you can change your life. She stands on the scripture **Romans 12:2, "Be not conformed to this world, but be ye transformed by the renewing of your mind."**

LaTonya is the co-author of the anthology, *Camouflage: Because I Wear a Smile, Stories of Courage & Triumph* with 13 other co-authors. She is a certified Life Coach and has a bachelor's degree from (WSSU) Winston-Salem State University and Master's in Adult Education, concentration in Community Counseling from (NCAT) North Carolina Agriculture and Technical State University. She has operated in an exquisite fashion jewelry business for over 4 years and has built a successful team of over 40 women across North Carolina and other states. LaTonya is known for her soft-spoken demeanor and empathetic, yet empowering personality. LaTonya is the mother of 3 adult children and 5 grandchildren. Most importantly, LaTonya is a child of the King.

Sometimes the strongest people are the ones who love beyond all faults, cry behind closed doors and fights battles that nobody knows about. It's time you invest in your dreams and goals.

I would love for you to stay in connected with me. Below is my contact information.

LaTonya Renee on all Social Media platforms

Email: www.transformu@latonyarenee.com

Web address: www.latonyarenee.com

Phone: 336-443-0182

Come be a part of my very informative, inspirational, and empowering face book community. www.bit.ly/TFUFBGroup

Putting yourself first doesn't mean *only* caring about yourself. It means having a grounded and realistic understanding that *you are your first and only locus of control.* You have to be rooted in that before there's any possibility of lending yourself to anybody or anything else. www.bit.ly/ChatwitMe

Both fear and faith demand you believe in something you cannot see. Have faith in the best outcome, instead of fear of the worst. Don't allow fear to keep you stuck, and afraid to start a new chapter in your life.

It's time to take action against fear! Don't stay stuck another year! www.bit.ly/FreemeReplay

Made in the USA
Middletown, DE
21 July 2024

57479574R00086